Spelling Kindergarten Edition

Baby Professor
Education Kids

Speedy Publishing LLC
40 E. Main St. #1156
Newark, DE 19711
www.speedypublishing.com

Copyright 2018

All Rights reserved. No part of this book may be reproduced or used in any way or form or by any means whether electronic or mechanical, this means that you cannot record or photocopy any material ideas or tips that are provided in this book.

Aa

 Ant

 Arm

 Acorn

 Airplane

Bb

 Bee

 Ball

 Butterfly

 Backhoe

Cc

 Cake

 Carrot

 Clock

 Cloud

Dd

 Dragonfly

 Diamond

 Donut

 Dolphin

Ee

Egg

Earth

Eggplant

Eagle

Ff

Frog

Flower

Flag

Fork

Gg

 Gumball

 Ghost

 Giraffe

 Gift

Hh

 Hand

 Heart

 House

 Hippopotamus

 Igloo

 Iguana

 Ice

 Ink

Jj

 Jam

 Jelly

 Jacket

 Jigsaw

Kk

 Koala

 Key

 Knife

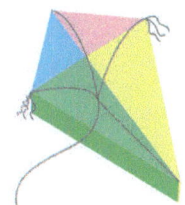 Kite

 Letter

 Lemon

 Leaf

 Ladybug

Mm

 Monkey

 Milk

 Meat

 Mushroom

Nn

 Nest

 Note

 Nail

 Notebook

Oo

 Octopus

 Orange

 Ostrich

 Orchid

Pp

 Pig

 Pencil

 Penguin

 Peacock

Qq

 Queen

 Quail

 Quilt

 Quill

Rr

 Robot

 Rainbow

 Ring

 Rocking horse

Ss

 Shirt

 Slide

 Snail

 Sun

Tt

 Tablet

 Turtle

 Tennis

 Tree

U u

 Unlock

 Unicorn

 UFO

 Underwear

Vv

 Van

 Violin

 Vase

 Volcano

Ww

 Watermelon

 Wagon

 Worm

 Weathercock

Xx

 Xylophone

 X-ray

Yy

 Yellow

 Yarn

 Yacht

 Yak

Zz

 Zebra

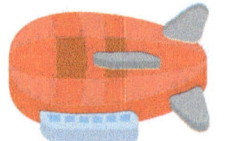 Zeppelin

 Zero

 Zucchini

Choose the correct letter to spell the word of the picture shown.

Z _ p p _ r

S _ r a _ b _ r _ y

R _ b _ it

D _ _ k

M _ _ n

Choose the correct letter to spell the word of the picture shown.

 D _ l _ h _ n

 U _ b _ e _ la

 A _ _ le

 Ne _ _ kl _ _ e

 T _ g _ r

Choose the correct letter to spell the word of the picture shown.

Y _ _ o

B _ _ k

L _ n

O _ l

C _ r

Printed by BoD"in Norderstedt, Germany